TATTY CAT AND THE WONDERFUL WHIFF

TATTY CAT AND THE WONDERFUL WHIFF

Written by
MELLA MAY

Illustrated by
GEORGE UTTON

First Published in 2023 by Fantastic Books Publishing
Cover design by Gabi
Cover artwork and poem illustrations
by George Utton

ISBN (ebook): 978-1-914060-53-3
ISBN (paperback): 978-1-914060-54-0

To Diana and Mervyn, thank you for your unwavering
support and belief in me over the years

The wind was up,
the breeze was strong,
The clouds of grey
were scudding along.

Tatty-Cat stretched
and sniffed at the air –
And breathed in a whiff,
so faint and rare…

A Wonderful Whiff,
that was wafting his way
A Wonderful Whiff –
Oh Hip, Hip, Hooray!
A Wonderful Whiff –
Oh boy, Oh boy!
A Wonderful Whiff –
Oh joy, Oh joy!

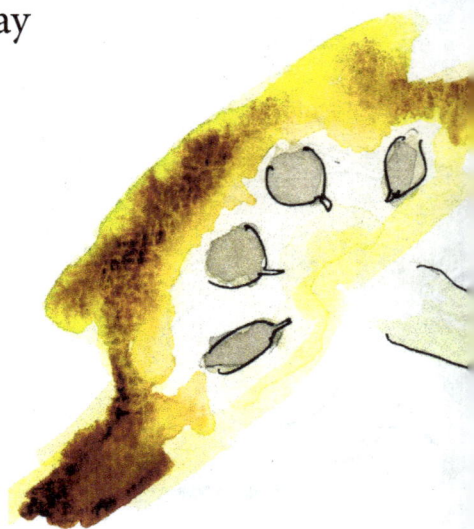

Standing quite still his nose all a-quiver,
Tatty-Cat swayed and began to shiver
Trembling with joy he jumped to his toes
And ran like the wind, to follow his nose…

Oh, where was that whiff
That was wafting along?
That amazing aroma,
That most pungent pong?

He just had to find it,
That much was plain,
Or that fabulous fragrance
Would drive him insane!

So he raced through the field
passed the old oak tree,
And followed the river,
laughing with glee.
Then he flew down a track –
avoiding a pond –
And came to the village
that lay beyond

Here at the village he tasted the air,
And inhaling the whiff, ran off like a hare.
Passed all the houses that lay by the wood,
And into the street just as fast as he could

Oh, where was that whiff
That was wafting along?
That amazing aroma,
That most pungent pong?

He just had to find it,
That much was plain,
Or that fabulous fragrance
Would drive him insane!

He came to some shops
set out in a row,
And paused for a moment –
which way should he go?
Closing his eyes he sniffed a great sniff
And then he was off –
to the Source of the Whiff!

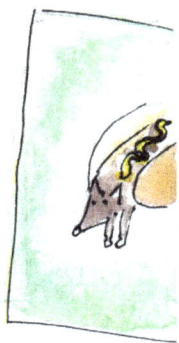

He ran to the door
of one little shop
Then raced round the back
with a skipperty-hop!
Outside in the yard
was a big smelly bin
And here was the place
where the Whiff did begin!

Oh, where was that whiff
That was wafting along?
That amazing aroma,
That most pungent pong?

He just had to find it,
That much was plain,
Or that fabulous fragrance
Would drive him insane!

He came to a stop,
and gazed at the bin –
Such treasures inside,
where should he begin?
With a great whoop of joy,
and so much to gain
He dived in head first,
his prize to obtain!

Oh, where was that whiff
That was wafting along?
That amazing aroma,
That most pungent pong?

He just had to find it,
That much was plain,
Or that fabulous fragrance
Would drive him insane!

Through ketchup stained napkins,
And vinegar drips,
He dug through the rubbish
And unwanted chips.

A bread roll all mouldy,
And half a fish cake
Were thrown on the ground
And strewn in his wake.

Three sachets of mustard,
And two cans of pop,
Were sent high in the air
To land with a PLOP!

Some old bits of batter
All greasy and brown
Were completely ignored
As he dug further down.

Oh, where was that whiff
That was wafting along?
That amazing aroma,
That most pungent pong?

He just had to find it,
That much was plain,
Or that fabulous fragrance
Would drive him insane!

Then finally he found it,
His glorious prize;
Which made his mouth water
And brought tears to his eyes.

Thrown out with the rubbish
To rot and decay,
Was this marvellous feast
Now heading his way!

Then all of a sudden
He became aware
Of others around him
All wanting a share!

He paused for a moment
And saw with a fright,
A small crowd had gathered
All seeking a bite!

There was old Scabby Tabby,
who's known to be tough
And Black and White Bertie,
who's equally rough.
Plus Amber and Oscar
and Siamese Su,
And the Tortoiseshell Triplets,
all in the queue!

Then there was Maddox the Manx,
with the scruffy old fur,
And Tinker the Moggie,
with a very loud purr.
And with Old Smokey Joe,
the Gang was complete –
Every cat in the village now
wanted his treat!

But more scary than that
was the Chip Shop's Big Boss
Who was Roaring and Shouting,
and looking quite cross
He jumped up and down
in his apron and hat
Which was very alarming
to a small Tatty-Cat

Deciding quite quickly
that this was not fun
Tatty-Cat reasoned
his best choice was…RUN!!
So grabbing his prize
tight in his jaw
He leapt from the bin
and down to the floor

In his haste to escape,
he knocked over the bin,
Which upset the Boss
and caused quite a din.
Then startled and shocked,
the other cats ran –
Which seemed at the time
a very wise plan

Tatty-Cat raced back
down the main street
And tore passed the shops,
still clutching his treat.
He ran passed the old houses
down by the wood,
And out of the village,
as fast as he could.

He flew to the fields
and marshes beyond
And back down the track –
avoiding the pond –
Then onto the river –
laughing with glee –
And back to his spot
by the Old Oak Tree

And here he flopped down,
and could run no more
Exhausted and tired,
with an ache in his jaw.
But alone now at last
with his tasty treat,
Tatty-Cat smiled
and prepared to eat.

Though now slightly battered
and worse for wear,
He regarded his prize
with the greatest of care;
Licking his lips
he began to tuck in
To the reward
he had fought so hard to win

Each mouthful he took
was just pure delight –
Such wonderful flavours
in every bite!
The meal without doubt
was the best he had eaten
And Tatty-Cat knew
it would never be beaten

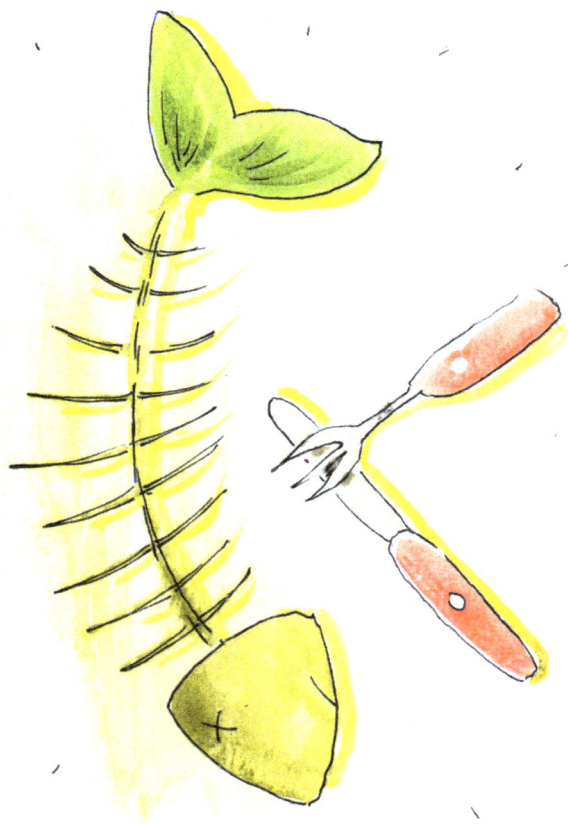

Then finally full
and purring with pleasure
He lay down to sleep
and dream of his treasure
Of the Wonderful Whiff
which had floated and swirled
And led to the most successful

Amazing,
  Marvellous,
    Foul-Smelling,
      Disgusting,
        Rotten,
          Slimy,
            Filthy,
              Stinky,

Fishing Trip in the World!

About the Author

Born in Northumberland and brought up in Wiltshire, Mella May left home in the late 1970's after finishing college and moved to London where she worked as a secretary for the BBC at Television Centre until the early 1980's before heading up to East Anglia and the Norfolk Broads to live. It was here that she married and raised her family and here that has been home for over 40 years along with the various rescue cats and dogs that have shared her life.

Mella has always enjoyed writing but it is only now in semi-retirement that she has had time to begin to take it up professionally – so still somewhat new to this whole world of publishing, but very much looking forward to the new adventure!

Mella enjoys reading, walking along the beach [in all weathers] pottering around the garden and spending time with her family and young grandchildren

Mella does not yet have a website but can be contacted through her Facebook page Mella May Stories

About the Artist

George Utton is a writer and illustrator based in Norwich where he primarily works at a local charity supporting children with disabilities. George moved to Norwich to study at the University of East Anglia and in 2018 he earned his MA in creative writing. He is currently looking to apply his script-writing skills in the world of radio, writing fictional short-stories and plays. He finds working with children extremely rewarding as he finds their unbridled imagination a constant source of inspiration. He also likes the fact it allows him the freedom to act like a big kid himself sometimes.

If you have enjoyed this book, please consider leaving a review on Amazon and Goodreads for Mella May and George Utton to let them know what you thought of their work.

These blank pages are for your own drawings of Tatty Cat, getting into all sorts of sticky, stinky situations

These blank pages are for your own drawings of Tatty Cat, getting into all sorts of sticky, stinky situations

These blank pages are for your own
drawings of Tatty Cat, getting into
all sorts of sticky, stinky situations

These blank pages are for your own
drawings of Tatty Cat, getting into
all sorts of sticky, stinky situations

These blank pages are for your own
drawings of Tatty Cat, getting into
all sorts of sticky, stinky situations

These blank pages are for your own drawings of Tatty Cat, getting into all sorts of sticky, stinky situations

These blank pages are for your own drawings of Tatty Cat, getting into all sorts of sticky, stinky situations

These blank pages are for your own drawings of Tatty Cat, getting into all sorts of sticky, stinky situations

These blank pages are for your own
drawings of Tatty Cat, getting into
all sorts of sticky, stinky situations

These blank pages are for your own
drawings of Tatty Cat, getting into
all sorts of sticky, stinky situations

These blank pages are for your own drawings of Tatty Cat, getting into all sorts of sticky, stinky situations

These blank pages are for your own
drawings of Tatty Cat, getting into
all sorts of sticky, stinky situations

These blank pages are for your own drawings of Tatty Cat, getting into all sorts of sticky, stinky situations

These blank pages are for your own
drawings of Tatty Cat, getting into
all sorts of sticky, stinky situations

These blank pages are for your own drawings of Tatty Cat, getting into all sorts of sticky, stinky situations

These blank pages are for your own drawings of Tatty Cat, getting into all sorts of sticky, stinky situations

These blank pages are for your own
drawings of Tatty Cat, getting into
all sorts of sticky, stinky situations

These blank pages are for your own drawings of Tatty Cat, getting into all sorts of sticky, stinky situations

These blank pages are for your own drawings of Tatty Cat, getting into all sorts of sticky, stinky situations

These blank pages are for your own drawings of Tatty Cat, getting into all sorts of sticky, stinky situations

These blank pages are for your own
drawings of Tatty Cat, getting into
all sorts of sticky, stinky situations

These blank pages are for your own drawings of Tatty Cat, getting into all sorts of sticky, stinky situations